$16.95

7/20/15

Mis cinco sentidos / My Five Senses

LO QUE HUELO/
WHAT I SMELL

By Alex Appleby   Traducción al español: Christina Green

Gareth Stevens
PUBLISHING

Please visit our website, www.garethstevens.com. For a free color catalog of all our high-quality books, call toll free 1-800-542-2595 or fax 1-877-542-2596.

Library of Congress Cataloging-in-Publication Data

Appleby, Alex.
What I smell = Lo que huelo / by Alex Appleby.
p. cm. — (My five senses = Mis cinco sentidos)
Parallel title: Mis cinco sentidos
In English and Spanish.
Includes index.
ISBN 978-1-4824-0872-0 (library binding)
1. Smell — Juvenile literature. 2. Senses and sensation — Juvenile literature. I. Appleby, Alex. II. Title.
QP458.A66 2015
612.8—d23

First Edition

Published in 2015 by
Gareth Stevens Publishing
111 East 14th Street, Suite 349
New York, NY 10003

Copyright © 2015 Gareth Stevens Publishing

Editor: Ryan Nagelhout
Designer: Andrea Davison-Bartolotta
Spanish Translation: Christina Green

Photo credits: Cover, p. 1 Martin Barraud/OJO Images/Getty Images; p. 5 (hand) Denys Prykhodov/Shutterstock.com; p. 5 (eye) Altin Osmanaj/Shutterstock.com; p. 5 (ear) hideous410grapher/iStock/Thinkstock; p. 5 (mouth) lovro77/iStock/Thinkstock; p. 5 (nose) Jani Bryson/iStock/Thinkstock; p. 7 wong sze yuen/Shutterstock.com; p. 9 stockphoto mania/Shutterstock.com; p. 11 Aprilphoto/Shutterstock.com; p. 13 (top left) Lars Koch/iStock/Thinkstock; p. 13 (top right) tashka2000/iStock/Thinkstock; p. 13 (bottom left) Paval_Hadzinski/iStock/Thinkstock; p. 13 (bottom right) rez-art/iStock/Thinkstock; pp. 15, 24 (apple pie) Dani Vincek/Shutterstock.com; pp. 17, 24 (flowers) Samuel Borges Photography/Shutterstock.com; p. 19 (top left) ZoneFatal/Shutterstock.com; p. 19 (top right) BananaStock/Thinkstock; p. 19 (bottom left) Catherine Yeulet/iStock/Thinkstock; p. 19 (bottom right) Stephen Gibson/Shutterstock.com; pp. 21, 24 (feet) Cappi Thompson/Flickr/Getty Images; p. 23 Ann Worthy/iStock/Thinkstock.

Printed in the United States of America

CPSIA compliance information: Batch #CS15GS: For further information contact Gareth Stevens, New York, New York at 1-800-542-2595.

Contenido

Contents

Me gusta usar
mis sentidos.

I like to use my senses.

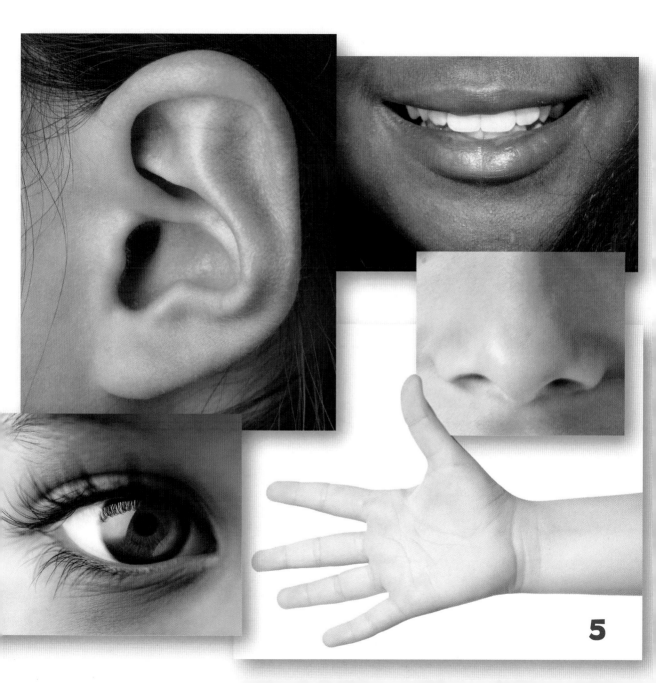

5

¡Me encanta oler!

I love to smell!

Huelo con la nariz.

I smell with my nose.

9

También la uso
para respirar.

I also use it to breathe.

11

¡Hay muchos
ricos olores!

There are lots
of good smells!

Me encanta el olor del
pastel de manzana.

I love the smell
of apple pie.

¡Las flores también huelen bien!

Flowers smell nice, too!

Otras cosas huelen mal.

Other things smell bad.

19

¡A veces mis
pies apestan!

Sometimes my
feet stink!

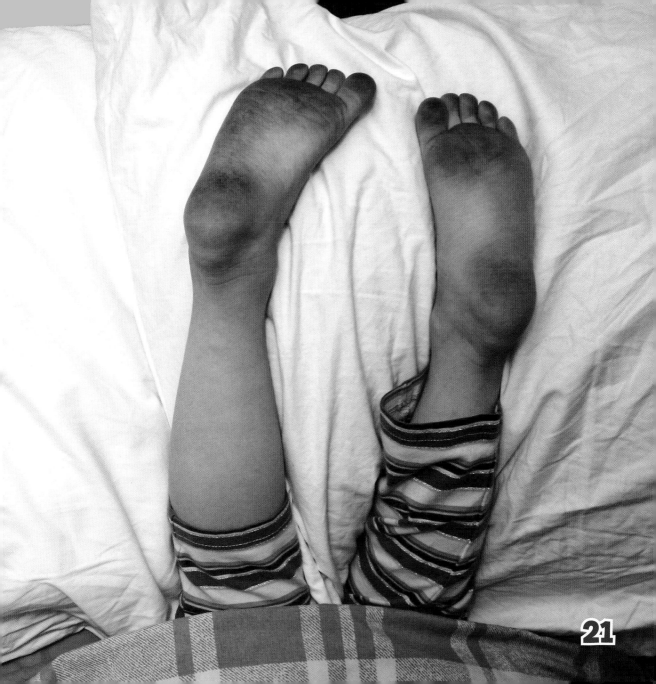

Es divertido oler
cosas nuevas.

It is fun to smell
new things.

Palabras que debes saber/ Words to Know

(el) pastel de manzana/ apple pie

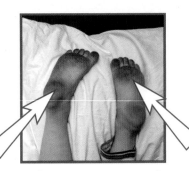

(los) pies/ feet

(las) flores/ flowers

Índice / Index